D0759294

Rookie
Read-About®
Science

It's a Good Thing There Are
Earthworms

by Jodi Shepherd

Content Consultant
Elizabeth Case DeSantis, M.A. Elementary Education
Julia A. Stark Elementary School, Stamford, Connecticut

Reading Consultant
Jeanne Clidas, Ph.D.
Reading Specialist

Children's Press®
An Imprint of Scholastic Inc.
New York Toronto London Auckland Sydney
Mexico City New Delhi Hong Kong
Danbury, Connecticut

Library of Congress Cataloging-in-Publication Data
Shepherd, Jodie, author.
It's a good thing there are earthworms/by Jodie Shepherd.
    pages cm. — (Rookie read-about science)
Summary: "Introduces the reader to earthworms and explains the roles they play
in the environment."— Provided by publisher.
Audience: Ages 3-6.
ISBN 978-0-531-22364-2 (library binding: alk. paper) — ISBN 978-0-531-22836-4 (pbk.: alk. paper)
    1. Earthworms—Juvenile literature. I. Title. II. Title: It is a good thing there are
earthworms. III. Series: Rookie read-about science.

QL391.A6S53 2015
592.64—dc23   2014014966

No part of this publication may be reproduced in whole or in part, or stored
in a retrieval system, or transmitted in any form or by any means, electronic,
mechanical, photocopying, recording, or otherwise, without written permission
of the publisher. For information regarding permission, write to Scholastic Inc.,
Attention: Permissions Department, 557 Broadway, New York, NY 10012.

Produced by Spooky Cheetah Press
Design by Keith Plechaty

© 2015 by Scholastic Inc.

All rights reserved. Published in 2015 by Children's Press, an imprint of Scholastic Inc.

Printed in China 62

SCHOLASTIC, CHILDREN'S PRESS, ROOKIE READ-ABOUT®, and associated logos
are trademarks and/or registered trademarks of Scholastic Inc.

1 2 3 4 5 6 7 8 9 10 R 24 23 22 21 20 19 18 17 16 15

Photographs ©: age fotostock/H Schmidbauer: 27 top left; Alamy Images: 3 top left,
11 (Arterra Picture Library), 31 top (Steve Gschmeissner/SPL); Animals Animals/David M. Dennis:
cover main; Corbis Images/David P. Hall: 30 bottom right; Dreamstime/Mikelane45: 23;
iStockphoto: 3 top right, 8 (James Brey), 20 (R_Koopmans); Ken Karp Photography: cover top;
Museum Victoria/Rodney Start: 28 center; Reuters/Henry Romero: 28 bottom; Science Source: 15,
28 top (Colin Varndell), 27 bottom (John Serrao), 12 top, 12 bottom (Phil Degginger), 19, 31 center
top (R. Konig/Jacana); Superstock, Inc.: 7, 27 top right (Derek Middleton), 16, 31 bottom (Minden
Pictures); Thinkstock: 30 top left (AKodisinghe), 3 bottom (Anatolii Tsekhmister), 30 top right
(HappyToBeHomeless), 29 top right (Mikhail Kokhanchikov), 4 (Vitaliy Pakhnyushchyy); Wikipedia/
Obsidian Soul: 24, 31 center bottom.

Table of Contents

4

It's a Good Thing...

Some people think earthworms are just garden pests. Others think these creepy-crawlies are just plain yucky! But it's a good thing there are earthworms!

Earthworms help plants grow as they tunnel through dirt. As they dig, the earthworms eat dead plants, seeds, roots, leaves, and dirt. They turn them into waste called pellets. Pellets make the soil extra healthy.

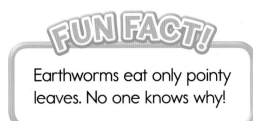

FUN FACT!

Earthworms eat only pointy leaves. No one knows why!

The earthworms' tunnels loosen the soil. Air and water come into the loose soil and help plants grow.

Earthworms are also food for birds, frogs, and other animals.

A robin feeds a worm to her chicks.

Earthworm Bodies

Earthworms have no bones and no legs. These useful critters get around by wiggling. Special rings around their bodies let them wiggle and move.

The rings on this worm's body help it move.

rings

mouth

To move, first the worms stretch out long and thin. Then they squeeze up short and fat. **Bristles** on their bodies help them grip the soil as they crawl.

Can *you* wiggle like an earthworm?

An earthworm repeats a two-step process to move.

Earthworms have tiny brains. They have no eyes and no ears. They do not have lungs either. They breathe in air through their skin.

Earthworms have mouths but no teeth. Look for the end of the worm that's wider. That's where the mouth is.

Can you guess where this earthworm's mouth is?

14

16

Gooey **mucus** covers the earthworms. It keeps their skin moist. It also helps them slide through the soil.

Shiny mucus keeps this earthworm healthy.

Where Do Earthworms Live?

Earthworms can live almost anywhere in the world, except where the ground is too dry or too frozen. Earthworms live in underground **burrows**.

FUN FACT!

In winter, earthworms sleep, or hibernate, deep underground.

Watch the ground after it rains. You may see lots of earthworms because the ground is wet. Usually it is hard for them to be aboveground. The sun is too strong. It may dry them out.

As soon as the ground dries, this earthworm will go back underground.

More and More Earthworms!

Earthworms come aboveground to mate, too. There are no male or female worms. Each worm is both male and female! But you still need two worms to make babies.

23

After the worms mate, they lay eggs. They use mucus to make a **cocoon**. The cocoon covers the eggs and keeps them safe inside.

When baby worms hatch, they are tiny and white. Then their skin turns dark. They are ready to get to work in the garden.

Earthworm eggs are tiny.

Now you know these hard-working garden critters help us in many ways. It's a good thing there are earthworms!

Earthworms Are Good For...

...making soil healthy.

...helping plants grow.

...providing food for animals like birds and frogs.

Creature

When an earthworm is cut in two, it may be able to regenerate, or grow, a new head or tail!

Most earthworms are small. One of the largest earthworms is the giant Gippsland earthworm. It lives in Australia and is 3 feet (0.9 meters) long.

In some countries, people eat earthworms—and like them!

Feature Fun

There are thousands of different kinds of earthworms, including red wrigglers (right) and night crawlers, which are used for fishing bait.

RIDDLES

Q. What do you get if you cross a worm with an elephant?

A. Very big holes in your garden!

Q. How can you tell which end of a worm is which?

A. Tickle in the middle and see which end laughs!

Creature Feature Fun

Which habitat is right for earthworms?

A

B

Answer: A. A garden is the perfect spot for earthworms to tunnel through the soil.

Be a Friend to Earthworms

Next time you see an earthworm on a sidewalk or driveway, do it a favor and move it to a shady spot. Ask an adult to help you pick up the worm *very gently* and place it in the grass, preferably under a tree or bush. Then it can safely tunnel its way back down into the soil.

Glossary

bristles (BRISS-uhls): stiff hairs on an earthworm's body that help it grip the soil

burrows (BUR-ohs): underground tunnels in which earthworms live

cocoon (kuh-KOON): covering made to protect eggs

mucus (MYOO-kuhss): gooey liquid that covers an earthworm's body

Index

Facts for Now

Visit this Scholastic Web site for more information on earthworms:
www.factsfornow.scholastic.com
Enter the keyword **Earthworms**

About the Author

Jodie Shepherd, who also writes under the name Leslie Kimmelman, is an award-winning author of dozens of books for children, both fiction and nonfiction. She is a children's book editor, too.